Sit Your Ass on the Potty

Written and illustrated

By

Candice Hyman

Copyright © 2015 Candice Hyman-thekhaidencehouse.com

All rights reserved. No part of this publication may be reproduced, distributed, or transmitted in any form or by any means, including photocopying, recording, or other electronic or mechanical methods, without the prior written permission of the publisher, except in the case of brief quotations embodied in critical reviews and certain other noncommercial uses permitted by copyright law.

Published by The Khaidence House Publishing Co.

info@thekhaidencehouse.com

ISBN-13: 978-0692454497
ISBN-10: 0692454497

DEDICATION

The dedication of this book belongs to my longtime friend Jamala. We have been taking on this world together for 24 years now! I am so thankful to have you as my friend, or should I call you, cousin? We'll have to ask your mom about that again! (LOL) But one thing that I do know is that I don't ever have to fret over what's lurking behind me because I know you have my back! This dedication from me represents the love, motivation and experience that we've shared.

With Sincerity and Appreciation.
Candice Hyman

COMING SOON

Mommy Don't Fall For Daddy's Shit

ACKNOWLEDGMENTS

I would like to thank my friends and family for your love and support! Your encouraging words became the food to my hunger to succeed and accomplish this goal.

You're incredibly bright, a prodigy I'm sure. But the expressions on your face say "why, what for?"

The manipulation technique is superb, and you have mastered being naughty. But at the age of two, it's time to sit your ass on the potty.

A technology Guru in the making, I'm so overjoyed and proud, to see you flip through my phone when I never taught you how. Then he started dialing numbers and said he's calling Kennedy? Well...if you can call her, you sure can sit your ass on the potty.

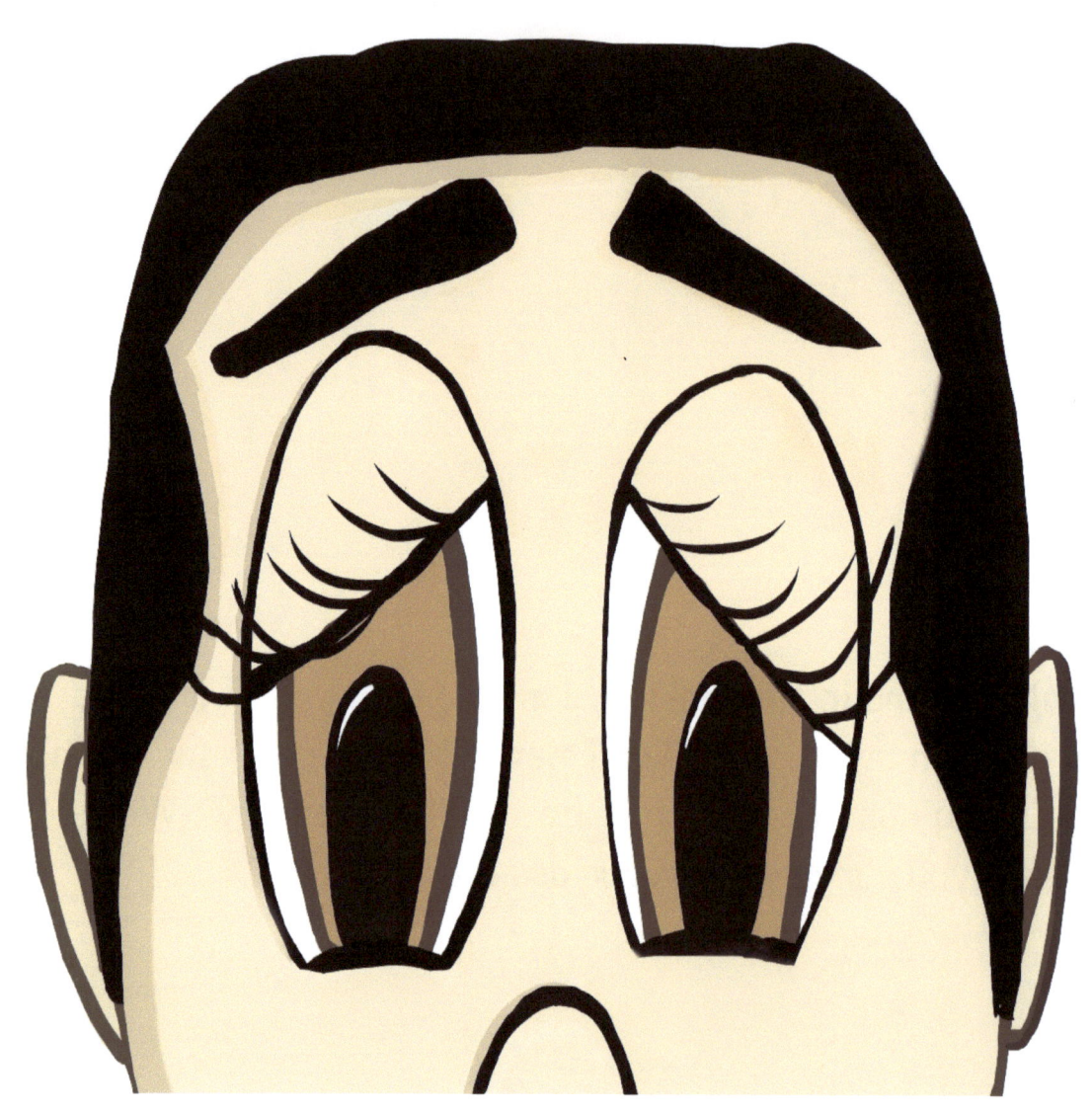

Your big brown eyes are trained to hypnotize. So you made me think you weren't ready the last time I made you try.

But then, you took the television remote controller and ordered "Beam Me Up Froggy"? Then I thought, "If you can do all that shit, you can sit your ass on the potty!"

Creative like an Author, wait... you can write "A- B- C"? If you can do that, you can write down "POTTY".

Look here my intellectual son! The smelly diapers have just got to go! Please don't drop another stinky bomb! Please, please no!

Why O why does he debate with me? A future lawyer, maybe? It's a possibility since he just used reverse psychology.

He ordered his food in the drive-thru, and then danced in the car seat. Khaidence said, mommy turn on my song, "Move Move Your Body"! With frustration he shouted! "Hey, you forgot, I want my tater totties!" I said, if you noticed all that shit, get your "kids meal" ass on the potty!

How can you kids be so talented with amazing gifts beyond belief, but you love to drive your parents freaking crazy?

So here comes daddy, stepping in to intervene. Then you sit right on the potty and take a long pee.

Oh really, you fooled me? You can wipe yourself too? "And the best Actors Award", goes straight to you!

Now that I have proof that you're fully capable of complying, don't you ever deceive me again or start lying! Just sixteen more years until college, then you'll find a jobbie, but for now come sit your ass on this potty.

The End

www.ingramcontent.com/pod-product-compliance
Lightning Source LLC
LaVergne TN
LVHW072058070426
835508LV00002B/162